AF609747

Savage Love
Carstens / Karlsson

First edition. Printed in the USA.

Poetry by Wolfgang Carstens
www.wolfgangcarstens.com

Art by Janne Karlsson
www.svenskapache.se

ISBN: 978-1-926860-51-0

Epic Rites Press publications are distributed worldwide by Tree Killer Ink. For more information about *Savage Love* (and other books and publications from Epic Rites Press) please visit the Epic Rites website at www.epicrites.org, or address Tree Killer Ink / Epic Rites Press: 33 Sioux Road, PO Box 80002 Woodbridge, Sherwood Park, Alberta, Canada T8A 5T4.

Library and Archives Canada Cataloguing in Publication

Carstens, Wolfgang, author
Savage love / Wolfgang Carstens ; Janne Karlsson, illustrator.

Poems.
ISBN 978-1-926860-51-0 (paperback)

I. Title.
PS8605.A77768S29 2015 C811'.6 C2015-907051-1

Epic Rites: any press is only as "small" as its thinking.

Contents

RISE, MOTHERFUCKER!!
IT'S THE POWER
OF CHRIST
THAT COMPELS YOU!!!
©J.K
-15

researching

my newest book,

i joined
an online penis enlargement forum.

a few weeks later,
they asked
if i wanted to join
their no-limit Hold 'Em team
at PokerStars.

now,
i ain't no rocket scientist

but no-limit poker
requires courage,
confidence –
ice
in your veins,

and
when the chips
are down,

the last place
in the world
i want to be
is on a team
with a bunch
of guys

with small dicks
and
no balls.

vaseline

"any man

who
gets with
me,"

she
said,

"has
to have
at least

eight
inches."

with
a ruler
in her
hands,

Vera

died
a
lonely
woman.

when he discovered

dirty pictures
on her phone,

Kenny thought
Vera was cheating
on him.

he was,
however,
mistaken.

it seems
he couldn't
recognize
his own dick

without
the ruler
pressed
against
it.

he never

quite understood
the difference
between

an umbilical cord
and
a penis

or why
that stupid doctor
had cut his
so bloody
short.

the only thing

Kenny remembered
about streaking
across the field
during halftime

were the two
blonde cheerleaders
at center field

pointing

and

laughing.

anything

over five inches
depressed him:

pickles,
carrots,
cucumbers,
sausages.

most especially
sausages.

Ron Jeremy

is quoted
as saying
"my cock
is so big

i see
the look
of fear
in women's
eyes."

it never
occurred
to him
his cock
was the
least

of their
worries.

"is there

a problem
with the desk fan,"
i asked,

as
i processed
the return paperwork.

"no, it's just
that my wife
doesn't think
six inches
is big enough,"
he said.

"they never
do,"

i muttered,

"they never
fucking
do."

it was worth

the fourteen bucks
just to see
the look
on her face
when he laid
the XXL condoms
on the checkout
counter.

besides,
Kenny reasoned,
it may
never happen
with Vera

and
he
could always
worry
about
the explanation
later.

SUPER
STORE

it was

at the annual
company Xmas blowout

when Kenny
opened the present
from Vera:

a ten inch cock sock
that resembled
an elephant.

it was followed
by everyone
chanting "put it on,
put it on!"

he was
taking it rather well
until
right there
in front of everyone,
Vera screamed

"don't worry, Kenny,
you can always
tie a knot
halfway
down
the trunk."

YOU HAVE
A SMALL PENIS,
SIR . . . ?
Janne
KARLSSON
-14

when Kenny

had
his penis
enhancement
surgery,

he
started
wearing
bicycle shorts

everywhere.

funny,

Kenny
didn't
own
a bike.

he knew

the jig
was up

when
Vera looked
at his
nakedness

and
quoted
his favorite line
from the movie
Jaws:

"i think
we're gonna
need

a
bigger
boat."

Ron Jeremy

is quoted
as saying
his true aspiration
is to become
a mainstream
movie actor.

when asked
about what kinds
of roles
he was interested
in looking at

Jeremy responded
simply:

"anything
that doesn't
require
me going
ass
to mouth."

Kenny

wore
his black
"choking hazard"
T-shirt

(with
the arrow
pointing
to his
crotch)

with pride
everywhere.

it wasn't
until Vera
pointed out
that it was
only the
smallest parts
that come with
a warning

that Kenny
finally
threw it
out.

CHOKING
HAZZARD

after three months

of taking the pills,
Kenny's dick hadn't
gotten any bigger.

his prostate,
however,
had swollen
to the size
of a grapefruit.

so much
for his motto
of trying anything
once.

"If I were
a blues musician,"
I said to my wife,
"I'd call myself
Slim Pickings."

My wife laughed,

then said,

"Or
if you ever
worked porno."

Strange.

i watch Dexter
and i want
to kill people.

i watch Mad Men
and i want to smoke,
drink, and screw
anything in a skirt.

Still,

i watch a Ron Jeremy porno
and all i want to do

is go on a diet.

if Ron Jeremy

has
taught us
anything,

it's that
it's better
to have
an average sized
penis,

than
to be fat,
ugly,
and gross.

most men

would probably agree
size matters:

no man,
after all,

wants
to be caught
in bed

with
a fat
woman.

"they actually

make male masturbators
shaped like flashlights

with vaginas
molded from famous
porn stars.

they're called
Fleshlights,"

that's crazy,
my wife said,

maybe
they should turn
my pussy
into one?

"i don't know,
baby,"
i said,

"i don't think
they make
lanterns."

Savage Love,

scene three:

it was
either
Ron Jeremy
pumping
Jenna Star

or
a white
rhinoceros

on
a paint
shaker.

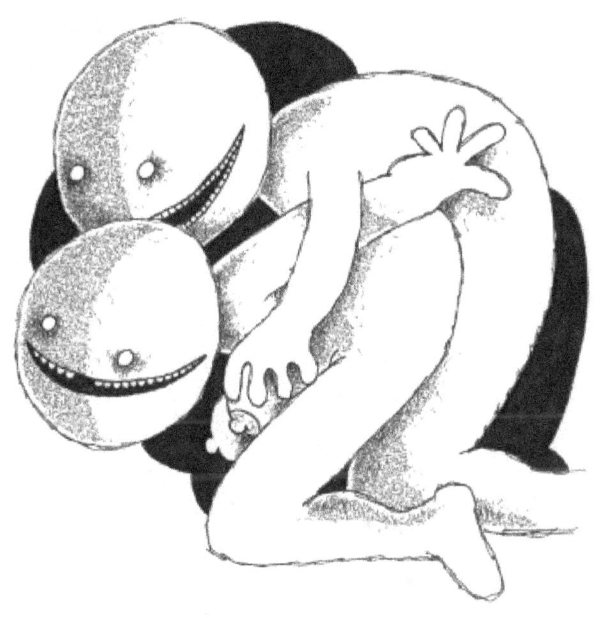

internet porn

has corrupted my mind.

today, for example,
the newspaper headline proclaimed:

Bruce Jenner spills guts on BBC.

now,
i don't know about you,
but, in my seedy world,
BBC is an acronym
for big black cock.

corrupted.

see
what i mean.

in one of his pornos,

Ron Jeremy
sucked
his own
cock.

illustrating
what philosophers
have known
for centuries:

size matters—

and that
when it comes
to brains

Ron Jeremy
has
a very small
one.

"you should try

rodeo,"

my wife
suggested,

"you're
a real pro

at
hanging on
for
eight
seconds."

he wanted

to remember
the gentleness
in her eyes,

the brightness
of her smile,

and the scent
of her flesh,

but
no matter
how hard he tried

nothing
could erase
the coldness
of her last words
right before
she put on
her clothes:

"those
were the seven
most awkward
seconds
of my life."

my wife and i

were down
at *The Fishin' Hole*
picking out new rods
for our trip.

"Honey,
come check
this one out,"
she screamed,
pointing at the slogan
on the handle,
"it's just like
you."

as i read
the words:
"the most sensitive
rod in the world,"
i just looked at her,

shook my head,

then said,

"don't
say
another
fucking
word."

$150
MAGGOTS

Michael Jackson

was
recently named
"the dirtiest,
most unsanitary
person
in Hollywood."

former porn star
Ron Jeremy
is rumored
to have reacted
to the allegations
against Jackson
by saying

"i
really dodged
a bullet
there."

when questioned
about where Jeremy
ranked on their survey,
Hollywood insiders
simply responded
with:

"Ron who?"

when asked

about
the documentary:
Porn Star:
The Legend
of Ron Jeremy,

celebrated film critic
Roger Ebert
is rumored
to have muttered,

"the film
is like Jeremy's
cock:

long

and

boring."

we were drunk

in the heart
of the Vegas strip
when we stumbled
into the piano bar.

it was in the middle
of the most gorgeous
Chopin concerto
when i realized
the pianist
was playing the keys
with his dick.

"holy shit, Honey,"
i said,

"that guy's cock
must be at least thirteen
fucking inches!"

my wife just chugged her beer,
laughed,
then said

"yeah,
and he plays
a better piano
than you
too!"

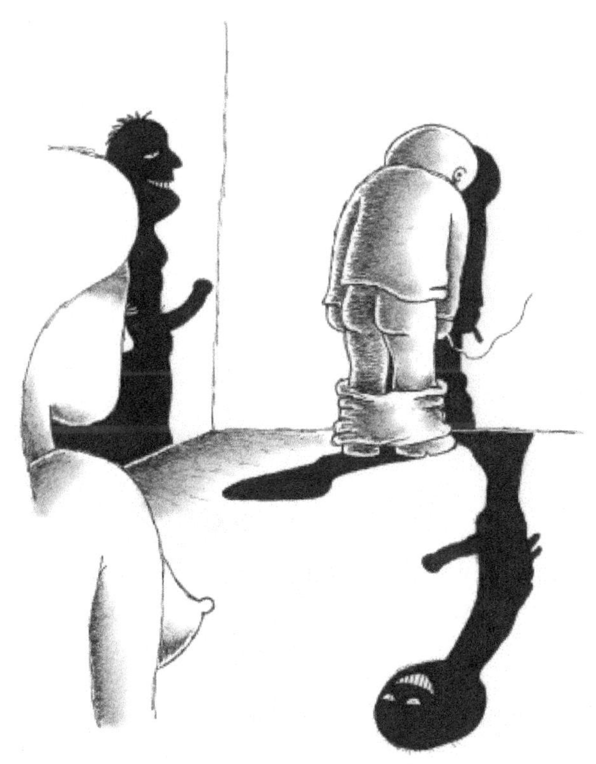

"it's hard

to explain,
Son,"
i said,

pulling down
my swim shorts,

"but
my dick
likes to hide."

"hide
from what?"
my son asked,
puzzled.

at this point
my wife
poked her head
in the dressing room,

yelling

"what the hell
is taking you guys
so goddamned long!"

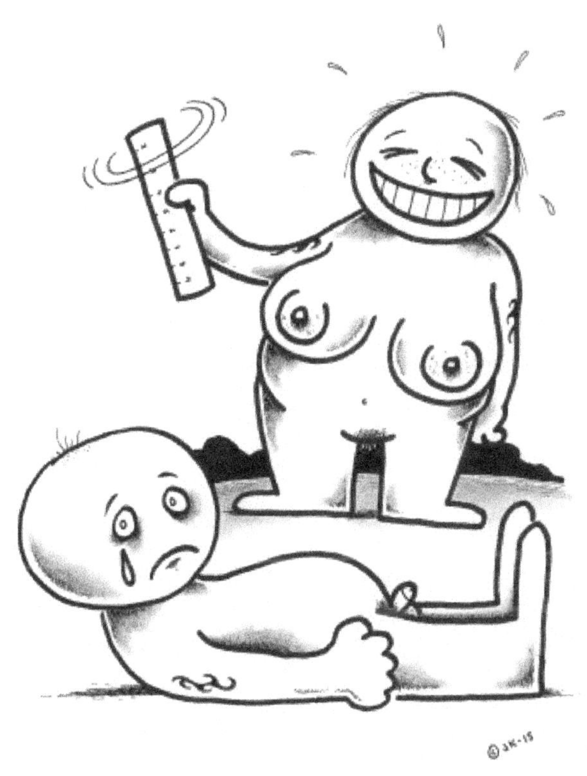
© JK-15

when asked why

Ron Jeremy
is nicknamed
"The Hedgehog,"

i explained
to my wife
it's because
he's overweight
and has
an abundance
of body hair.

"oh,"
she says,

"i thought
it had something
to do
with his penis."

you can nickname
my penis
if you want,
i offer.

my wife
thinks
for a minute,
then says,

"i think
i'll call it
The Turtle."

gee
thanks,
Bitch.

"look, Honey,"

i said,

holding up
the package
of Grace's
Cock Flavored
Soup,

"it's
your favorite
snack."

my wife
just looked at me,
laughed,
then said,

"if you didn't
feed me
such small
meals,

i wouldn't need
to snack
in-between."

we were at

the Bonnyville County Fair
watching a crappy magician
juggle chainsaws.

he asked for a volunteer
from the audience,

then pulled the redneck
sitting next to us
up on stage.

you
could literally
feel the women in the audience
gasp
at the massive bulge
in his jeans.

my wife
leaned in close
and whispered,

"do you think
his jeans
could get
any tighter?"

i couldn't blame her
for noticing,
of course,

but
the experience
only confirmed
what i already
knew:

i
fucking
hate
magic.

"i

already checked,"

my wife said,

as i read
the directions
on the box
of Miracle Grow,

"and

it doesn't
work

for
that. "

Protagoras

may be correct
in his assertion
that "man is the measure
of all things,"

yet,
until the measure of man
is determined,

all measurement
is meted out
in ignorance.

"if

it's
the little things
in life

that bring
the most
happiness,"

my wife said,

"then clearly
i'm one lucky
girl."

it's a sad commentary

when happiness
should be reduced
to the size of a muscle—

and sadder still
when the size of the muscle
in question
isn't the heart.

WOLFGANG CARSTENS

lives in Canada
with his five kids, wife,
grandson, dog, mortgage,
and death.

His poetry is printed
on the backs of unpaid bills.

More information at
wolfgangcarstens.com

JANNE KARLSSON

is a Swedish artist
who uses pens as therapy.
His dark, twisted art is
widely spread over the globe.

More information at
Svenskapache.se

www.ingramcontent.com/pod-product-compliance
Ingram Content Group UK Ltd.
Pitfield, Milton Keynes, MK11 3LW, UK
UKHW020236250726
13967UKWH00001B/401

9 781926 860510